DIRT

Poor planet Ea̶ t has given support t̶ ̶ects, animals and h̶ real trouble. Dirty g̶ ated and they're caus̶ ̶y great monsters with strange names like DEFORESTATION, TOXIC POLLUTION and GLOBAL WARMING. Luckily there are people in the world who know how to stop these monsters from destroying our planet. You can be one of those people too. By reading this Young Puffin Fact Book you'll be able to find out how the monsters were created and just what you can do to help fight back.

Christina and Alex Martinez are married with two children. Christina has worked as a journalist. Since 1986 she has helped Friends of the Earth on a number of children's projects, including setting up and running the EARTHWORM book award, writing and directing programmes of environmental education at London's Ecology Centre and Natural History Museum, and editing *Once Upon a Planet*, a Puffin collection of green stories.

Alex was born in Spain but has lived in London since he was four. He has also worked as a journalist, and is now a freelance teacher and writer.

Dirty Great Monsters

Our Planet in Trouble

Christina and Alex Martinez

Illustrated by
Heather Clarke

Puffin Books

For Raoul and Francesca

PUFFIN BOOKS

Published by the Penguin Group
Penguin Books Ltd, 27 Wrights Lane, London W8 5TZ, England
Penguin Books USA Inc., 375 Hudson Street, New York, New York 10014, USA
Penguin Books Australia Ltd, Ringwood, Victoria, Australia
Penguin Books Canada Ltd, 10 Alcorn Avenue, Toronto, Ontario, Canada M4V 3B2
Penguin Books (NZ) Ltd, 182–190 Wairau Road, Auckland 10, New Zealand

Penguin Books Ltd, Registered Offices: Harmondsworth, Middlesex, England

First published 1992
10 9 8 7 6 5 4 3 2 1

Filmset in 14 on 15pt Century Schoolbook

Printed in England by Clays Ltd, St Ives plc

Contents

Although you can find out about any one problem by turning to the chapter on it, no one problem can be fully understood by reading about it on its own. All the problems are linked. You will only see how they link up if you start at the beginning of the book and read on.

CHAPTER 1

Over-population

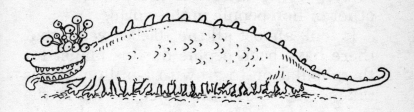

Have you noticed how crowded many shops and streets are? Have you ever had to wait a long time at a bus-stop because all the buses are full of people? And when at last you *have* got on a bus, has it often been stuck in miles of traffic? If the answers to these questions are 'yes', then you have already seen for yourself that too many people in the same place at the same time is a problem.

Over-population means too many people living on the Earth at the same time. The Earth is becoming over-populated – there are now more than 5 billion people. If we all held hands, the chain of people would go around the world 200 times and it would take 830 years to count every person!

The 'chain' is getting longer by the second – 150 babies are born every minute. An hour from now, 9,000 more will have been born. By the time you are old enough to stop going to school there will be another billion people in the world.

It took almost all the 100,000 years that there have been people on this planet for the population to grow to 1 billion. It has taken only 160 years since then for the number of people to grow to 5 billion. In forty years' time there could be double the number of people that there are now.

100,000 YEARS AGO

1000 YEARS AGO

160 YEARS AGO

TODAY

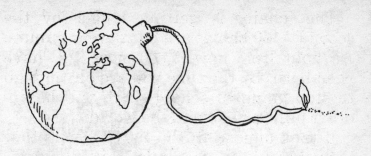

What has happened in the last 160 years is called a **population explosion**.

Bang!

The population explosion began when machines were first used on farms and in factories in Europe and North America. These machines were first built and used in Britain during a time that we now call the **Industrial Revolution**. For the first time in our history, food, clothes and furniture (and all the other things that people need and want) could be grown or made more quickly. Towns grew up around the factories as more and more houses were built for the thousands of poor people who had come from the countryside looking for work.

At first, the factory workers lived in overcrowded houses that had no clean water or proper toilets. Because of this, many people died young from illnesses like

9

typhoid and cholera. Most families were so poor that children had to work too. Some of these children died because their work was so hard, dirty and dangerous. Parents had lots of babies – it was not unusual to have ten, or even twenty children in one family! One of the reasons for this was to make sure that at least some of them would live long enough to grow up and help look after their parents when they got old.

As the years passed, the countries that used machines had more things to sell and became richer than those without machines. These richer countries (today called **developed countries**) decided to use some of their money to build cleaner towns and make new medicines. Soon, grown-ups started to live longer and, even though a lot of babies and children were still dying, the population of richer countries grew very fast.

As more and more houses with clean water and proper toilets were built, and children were not sent out to work any more, more boys and girls lived long enough to grow up and have their own babies. But for a long time, parents carried on having big families. One reason for this was that they could still remember the days when so many died very young.

Then, around the time your grandparents were born, people got used to the idea that they did not need to have such big families any more. At last the population explosion in Europe and North America came to an end.

But as it came to an end in one part of the world, it started in other places. People in African, Asian and South American countries began using new machines and medicines, and building cities, factories and roads. Today they are having a population explosion like the one that first happened in rich countries.

The population explosion in these and other poor countries (today called **developing countries**) is still going on.

WHY OVER-POPULATION IS DANGEROUS

Pollution is any dirt or poison that gets into the air, water or land. A lot of pollution comes from factories, cars and other things that people make. So more people means more pollution – and pollution is dangerous.

Because people need land for growing food and building homes, factories and roads, more people also means less natural, wild places. In the last 200 years we have destroyed thousands of kilometres of woods, forests and countryside. Many animals now have nowhere to live and are dying out. But as you will see later, we need trees, plants and animals to keep the planet and ourselves healthy. We cannot go on for ever taking up more land because we will soon run out of space. When that happens, we will not be able to grow enough food to feed everyone. Millions of people could starve.

The population is getting bigger but the Earth is not. Everything that you see around you in your town or city is made from things that came from the Earth. Sooner or later, some of these things, like metals, will run out. Many of the things you see around you are made by machines using fuel that comes from the Earth. Fuels

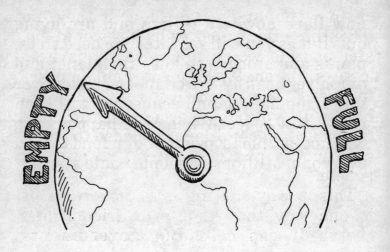

like oil, gas and coal *are* running out. It took the Earth nearly 20,000 years to make all the fuel that people now use up in just one week. The more people there are, the quicker we will use up these things. There is only so much that the Earth can give us.

SHARING IS THE ANSWER

If you have ever bought a clown's red nose on Comic Relief Day, or a Band Aid record at Christmas, or shopped at an Oxfam shop, you have already started sharing because the money you spent is sent to help people in poor countries. They need all the help and money they can get because many of them do not have homes, clean water or enough food. If they did have these things, fewer babies would die, and parents would not need to have so many children. Without our help, families in developing countries will carry on having lots of babies because so many of them die, and children are needed to work, earn money and look after sick and old people.

This is why sharing is so important. It is one way that you, your friends and everybody can help. But **governments** (the people in charge of a country) can help even more. Rich governments can help stop the population explosion by sharing their money and **technology** (new ideas and inventions) with poorer governments.

At the moment, people in Britain and the USA have, use up and waste about thirty times more than people in many African or South American countries.

Sharing would mean that the 1 billion people who live in richer countries (who now have too much) would have enough, and that the 4 billion people who live in developing countries (who now have too little) would also have enough. If we do not start sharing, then the dangers of over-population mean that, one day, there might not be enough for any of us.

CHAPTER 2

Sewage

Sewage is what we flush down our toilets. It is dirty, smelly and dangerous. Nasty germs grow on it. No wonder we do not want it anywhere near us! So every day billions of litres of sewage are flushed out of our homes and into underground tunnels called **sewers**. Some sewers are over 100 years old, are crumbling away, and are full of rats that feed on sewage and carry dangerous germs.

In some rich countries, a lot of sewage is 'cleaned' before it is allowed into lakes, rivers and seas. But in Britain, for example, 150 million bucketfuls of it are still poured straight into the sea every day.

Developing countries often do not have enough money to 'clean' their sewage, and so it is difficult for them not to pollute their water.

In the chapter about over-population you saw how people got sick and died when they lived in homes with dirty water and no proper toilets. The same thing happens to millions of fish, whales, dolphins and other animals when *their* homes (rivers, lakes and seas) are turned into giant 'toilets' for *our* sewage.

When a lot of sewage is poured into water it is like spreading horse-manure on a field to help plants grow. It makes water plants start growing thicker and stronger than before. Soon, they take up all the space. Germs also feed on sewage, and use up all the air in the water – this leaves none for the fish to breathe, and so they die. This is exactly what happened in the Great Lakes of North America about thirty years ago. Now their sewage is 'cleaned' first.

In July 1986, millions of fish died when a lot of sewage was pumped into the River Thames in Britain. A quarter of Britain's sewage goes straight into the North Sea, which could soon be empty of all life except germs. Some scientists think that all North Sea fish and other animals will have died in just two years' time if Britain does not start 'cleaning' more of its sewage.

Just like a boomerang comes back when you throw it, the problem of sewage comes back to us when we throw *it* away without 'cleaning' it first.

Sewage in food

One way it comes back is in the food we eat. We are using rivers, lakes and seas as 'toilets' and 'kitchens' at the same time. This means that we end up eating fish that have been made ill by our own sewage. Then we get ill too, and so do the animals that feed on them.

In 1988, the biggest seller of frozen food in Germany decided to stop selling nearly all fish caught in the North Sea because so many of the fish are sick.

Sewage in drinking-water

If sewage gets into our drinking-water it makes us very ill. Every hour, over 1,000 children in developing countries die of diarrhoea after drinking or washing in dirty water. Every year, over 25 million people die from illnesses like typhoid and cholera, which are spread by dirty water.

Sewage on beaches

More people are coming back from beach holidays feeling ill with ear infections, tummy upsets and flu. Very dangerous germs like hepatitis, polio and meningitis are also being found in polluted waters used for swimming by people on holiday.

Sewage from animals in factory farms

A 'factory farm' is a farm where many animals are packed together in a small space, and a lot of the work is done by machines. Many pigs, young cows and chickens are never allowed outside. Millions of people in rich countries buy lots of meat and milk, so farmers are keeping more animals in factory farms than ever before.

The 'sewage' from these animals is called **slurry**. Farmers dig deep holes in the ground to put it in, but quite often it runs out of cowsheds and pigsties or is washed out of the **slurry pits** by rain. Then it runs into nearby rivers and streams, poisoning and killing fish and the animals that feed there – just like our own sewage.

Sewage in streets

There is another kind of animal sewage that you might not think of as pollution. You probably see it in the street every day. When it gets on your shoes it brings germs and bad smells into your home. If it gets inside your body or into your eyes it can make you go blind. Have you guessed what it is yet? The answer is dog droppings. Our streets and parks are being

used as dog toilets. It is not the dog's fault, of course. All owners should scoop up their dog's dirt and get rid of it safely.

MAKING SEWAGE SAFE AND USEFUL

Long ago, when almost everybody lived in small villages dotted around the country-side, sewage was not the problem it is today. Because there were fewer people, there was not enough of it to poison large lakes and seas. But as villages grew into towns, smaller ponds and rivers nearby *did* get polluted by sewage because there were larger numbers of people living to-gether.

Wherever there are lots of people living in large towns or cities it is very important to have good, safe sewers. You can't make sewers safe yourself, but you can write a letter to the government asking it to build new sewers before the old ones become unsafe, and saying that you think all sewage should also be 'cleaned' before it

gets into the water. There are special places called **sewage works** that can do this. Although they cost money to build, they are cheap to run because sewage gives off a gas called **methane** that can be burnt as a fuel to power the cleaning machines.

Some villages in poorer countries are making sewage safe and useful in a different way. They are building special places under the ground called **biogas chambers** like the one in this picture. The methane gas given off by sewage and animal droppings is collected and used as a fuel to run machines, lamps and cookers.

Once sewage has been 'cleaned' in a sewage works or used to make fuel in a biogas chamber it can be spread on fields as a **fertilizer** (like horse-manure) to help food and plants grow.

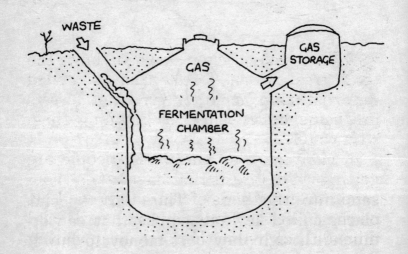

WASTE

GAS STORAGE

GAS

FERMENTATION CHAMBER

CHAPTER **3**

Deforestation

When people chop down or burn the trees in a forest this is called **deforestation**. Another way that forests are being destroyed is by flooding them with water.

In many parts of the world, people are getting rid of forests that have taken thousands, even millions of years to grow. Lots of the insects, plants, flowers, birds and animals that live in them are disappearing for ever too.

If people do not stop soon, there will be very few forests left in the world – then we will be in serious trouble.

25

TREES ARE MAGIC!

All over the world, for almost as long as there have been people, there have been stories about a magical 'tree of life'. No wonder people thought trees were magical, because:

- *trees help us to breathe*
  Did you know that the air you breathe out is different to the air you breathe in? Trees take in the **carbon dioxide** gas that people and animals breathe out and turn it into the **oxygen** we breathe in to stay alive. Just one beech tree makes enough oxygen to keep ten people alive!

- *trees take dirt out of the air*
  A group of elm trees about the size of a school playing-field can take as much as 5 tonnes of dirt out of the air in one year – that is the weight of an elephant!

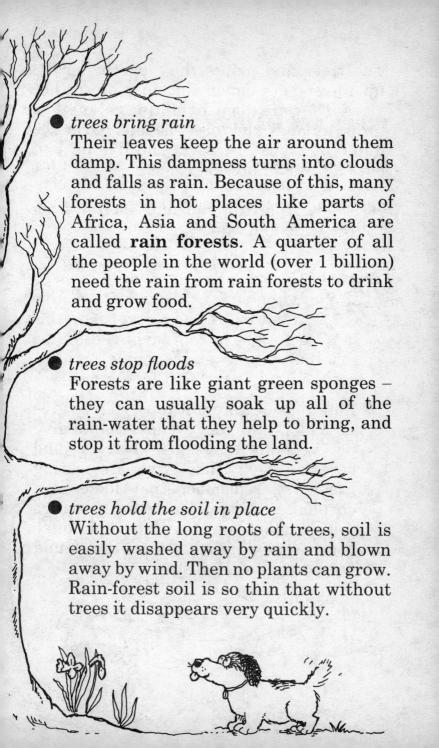

● *trees bring rain*
Their leaves keep the air around them damp. This dampness turns into clouds and falls as rain. Because of this, many forests in hot places like parts of Africa, Asia and South America are called **rain forests**. A quarter of all the people in the world (over 1 billion) need the rain from rain forests to drink and grow food.

● *trees stop floods*
Forests are like giant green sponges – they can usually soak up all of the rain-water that they help to bring, and stop it from flooding the land.

● *trees hold the soil in place*
Without the long roots of trees, soil is easily washed away by rain and blown away by wind. Then no plants can grow. Rain-forest soil is so thin that without trees it disappears very quickly.

The trees and plants that together make up forests are important in many other ways. They are home to millions of insects, birds, animals and forest people. (Over 240 different kinds of insects can live on just *one* oak tree!) Forests give us:

● shade from the sun and shelter from the wind and rain.

● hundreds of different foods. Trees give us fruits, nuts and syrups. Plants give us vegetables, beans, berries and cereals. Next time you are eating breakfast, remember that foods like cornflakes, crispy-rice cereals, orange juice, sugar, hot chocolate and coffee come from plants that were first found growing in rain forests.

● wood for building.

● firewood.

● other fuels. One petroleum nut-tree in Asia can make a litre of oil in a week. Imagine how much more oil a whole forest makes! The oil is used as a fuel for cooking and heating.

● rubber for tyres, rubber gloves, toys, balls, and so on.

- thousands of medicines. The chinchana tree, for example, gives us quinine, which can be used to treat an illness called malaria. Plants like the rosy periwinkle help cure blood cancer (**leukaemia**) in children. Scientists think that there are over 1,000 rain-forest plants that could cure many other kinds of cancer. One out of every four medicines sold in chemist's shops comes from rain-forest trees and plants.

- thousands of drugs that take away pain, stop bleeding, relax muscles, put us to sleep for operations, and so on.

● lots of enjoyment. They are beautiful to look at and fun to climb or explore.

DEFORESTATION AND DISAPPEARING WILDLIFE

Much of Europe and North America used to be covered in huge, old forests. As the numbers of people, towns and factories grew bigger, the forests were cut down for wood, firewood and farmland, and so they got smaller. Now there are very few left and they are in danger from acid rain (see chapter 4). Many of the insects, birds, plants and animals that lived in them have almost disappeared too – the buffalo in North America and the wolf, beaver, bear and purple emperor butterfly in Europe are a few examples.

Now that these rich countries have so few forests of their own left, they are using up forests in developing countries, and these are disappearing very fast. Imagine how many trees can grow in a space the

size of a football pitch – that is how many rain-forest trees are destroyed every second. Every hour, one kind of rain-forest animal, insect or plant is made **extinct**. Extinct means that the last one has died or been killed; there are none left in the world, and there will never be any more.

Millions of plants, insects and animals we know very little about are becoming extinct before we have had a chance to learn anything about them. Many other well-known animals are almost gone for ever because deforestation is destroying their homes, and people are hunting them.

Elephants. In the past ten years, half of all African elephants have been killed, leaving only about 600,000. Elephants are hunted for their ivory tusks, which are sold to be made into things like jewellery.

Tigers. There are only 8,000 Asian tigers left in the world. Tigers are hunted for their skins, which are sold as rugs.

Gorillas. There are about 400 mountain gorillas left living in the wild. They are hunted for meat. Their large heads and hands are sold for decoration.

Rhinos. They are hunted for their horns, which are made into powder and sold as a kind of medicine to people who think it makes them stronger. But it does not make them stronger. Rhino horns are made of the same stuff as our nails. There are just twenty-five northern white rhinos living wild in nature.

Pandas. So few giant pandas are left in the world that they are nearly extinct.

WHY HAVE HALF THE WORLD'S RAIN FORESTS GONE IN JUST FORTY YEARS?

The main reasons are:

Cattle-ranching for cheap beef

Huge areas of rain forest are burnt by cattle farmers called **ranchers** to clear land for their farms. Grass is planted and cattle are brought in to grow fat quickly. Then the cattle are killed, and beef is sold cheaply, mainly to rich countries, where it is eaten as steaks and hamburgers.

After two or three years, the thin rain-forest soil has no goodness left in it. No more grass can grow, and the land turns into a dry, cracked desert. The cattle-ranchers burn down another part of the forest, move their cattle, and start all over again. Rain-forest fires are so enormous that they can be seen from outer space.

Logging

Many rain-forest trees like mahogany, teak and ebony are much harder and stronger than **softwoods** like pines that grow in cooler countries. Because of this, lots of **hardwood** trees are being cut down by **loggers**. The hardwood is then sold to rich countries around the world, where it is made into furniture, window-frames or saucepan handles.

The trouble is that the loggers hardly ever plant any new trees. Only tree stumps are left. Rain-forest plants that need the shade of the trees soon die in the hot sun. The soil dries out and the land becomes desert.

Firewood

Many developing countries are very hot. The heat helps dangerous germs grow quickly on raw food. Cooking the food kills these germs, but many people in developing countries do not have money to buy fuel for cooking. Women and children walk a long way every day looking for sticks and firewood in forests. Their governments and factories also use millions of trees for fuel. Nearly half of all the wood cut in the world every year is used as firewood in developing countries.

Trees are being cut down for firewood quicker than they can grow back. Forests are getting smaller as the number of people needing firewood gets bigger. Already, there are more than 125 million people in these countries who cannot find or buy any firewood.

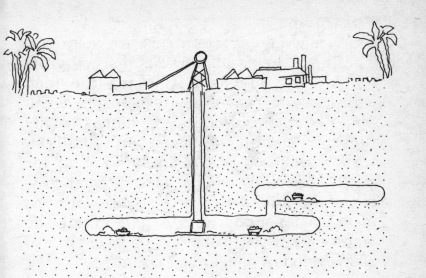

Mining

In the earth under the rain forests there are metals (like tin and gold), stones (like diamonds and emeralds), and oil. Many people want to buy these things, so miners dig deep down to get them out. Before they can build their mines, they have to burn away huge areas of forest. When the miners are working, poisonous metals (like **mercury**) are often washed into rivers, killing forest people and animals.

Many of these mines belong to business people in rich countries. They are allowed to mine because they have paid money to the governments of developing countries.

Roads and farming

Although the rain forests are very thick, the forest people who have lived in them for thousands of years know how to get about without destroying them. But people from the outside chop down the forest to make roads. The business people in charge of mines pay for these roads to be built deep into the rain forest. The roads are used for driving food and building materials to miners, cattle-ranchers and loggers. Metals, stones, oil, hardwood and beef are driven along these roads to ships and planes far away.

Five hundred million poor people in rain-forest countries around the world have no farmland or jobs, so they use the roads to get into the forest. These people clear away even more trees to make farms and grow food for their families.

The roads also bring something else into the forest – germs from the outside world. Illnesses like measles, that our bodies have learnt to fight, are new to the forest people. *Their* bodies do not yet know how to fight these illnesses so thousands of them have died and many more could die.

Flooding

When forests are cleared for cattle-ranches, logging, firewood, mining, roads or farming, the land becomes hard and dry. There are no trees or plants left to 'soak up' rain-water. The rain runs off the hard ground and into rivers, which often overflow, flooding villages, towns or cities. People and animals are drowned and many homes are lost.

But there is another kind of flooding that is being done on purpose – the reason is electricity. Electricity can be made by using the power of tonnes of moving water to turn special machines called **turbines**. First, the governments of some developing countries build giant 'walls' across rivers. The river water gets higher and higher until it spills out over miles and miles of rain forest. This drowns the forest and many of the things that live in it. The water pushes through special holes in the wall where the turbines are. These river walls are called **hydroelectric dams**.

In the next twenty years, the government of Brazil, in South America, is planning to build seventy-nine more dams in the rain forest. The dams will destroy forest land the size of Scotland and Wales put together. But if the dams that Brazil

already has were used more carefully, they would make more electricity and no new dams would have to be built.

SAVING THE FORESTS

If you think about it, all the different people that you have just been reading about are destroying the rain forests either **1** to stay alive, or **2** to earn a lot of money.

1 The people who destroy forests to stay alive have no other way of getting food, firewood, or of making a living for their families. As with the problem of over-population, sharing is the answer. With the help of governments and people in rich countries, poorer governments would have enough money and technology to give their many poor and starving people ways of staying alive without destroying the forests.

2 The people who destroy forests to sell things that come from them are not poor or starving. If they had to, they *could* do something else to earn money. We can help them to understand this by writing to them and explaining that the oxygen, clean air, rain, food, shelter, fuel, medicines and animals that forests give us are much more important.

We can also help them to understand this by not buying the things they are selling. Every one of us can live without so much meat, hardwood furniture, precious stones and metals, jewellery, and so on. But not one of us can live without forests.

CHAPTER **4**
Acid Rain

People, animals and plants need water to stay alive and healthy. You only have to think of a desert to realize what happens when there is too little water. Because of this, rain seems almost magical to many people who live in hot, dry countries. So you can imagine the shock that these people would feel if somebody told them that a lot of the rain that falls in some countries is killing living things. But it is true, and this 'killer' is called **acid rain**.

Acid rain attacks:

● *trees*

It eats away at leaves and gets deep inside all kinds of trees. Once there, it stops them from taking in goodness and water from the soil. Trees need **magnesium** and **calcium** to stay healthy, but acid rain washes these minerals out of the soil. It also lets loose a poisonous metal in the soil called **aluminium** that trees then drink in through their roots. Once trees have been attacked by acid rain they grow so weak that they cannot fight off germs or stay alive for very long in hot, dry weather.

Next time you are in a wood, forest or park, you will know that acid rain has attacked if you see:

● yellowing leaves or pine-needles;

● branches growing in strange shapes;

● few leaves at the top of the tree.

In Britain, more than half the trees are sick. Even more are sick in countries like Switzerland, Holland, Germany, Czechoslovakia and Poland. In some places, whole forests have died.

● *wildlife*
When aluminium in the soil is washed into lakes and rivers it poisons water plants and fish. Salmon and trout are disappearing fast. Many birds and animals (like the osprey, goosander and otter) which feed on fish cannot find enough food and starve to death.

Hundreds of lakes in Britain are under attack. In Sweden, 4,000 lakes are already empty of wildlife. Wildlife in 20,000 other lakes is disappearing. The same thing is happening in many other parts of Europe and North America.

● *people*

Like other kinds of pollution, acid rain is slowly poisoning our air and water. Today, more people than ever suffer from breathing problems and illnesses like asthma. Two million people in Britain now have this dangerous illness. In 1952, 4,000 people in London died in one week from a deadly mixture of fog, smoke and fumes that covered the city. It was a kind of acid rain, known in those days as **smog**.

More people seem to be getting aluminium poisoning too. Like other poisonous metals, aluminium damages the brain and nerves. People tremble and shake, and lose their memories.

● *buildings*

Acid rain even eats into stone and brick. During the 1980s, it actually made holes in many buildings in one city in Canada. Their bricks became

as soft as rubber. The Statue of Liberty in New York and St Paul's Cathedral in London are also being eaten away. All over the world many other beautiful buildings are under attack.

WHAT MAKES RAIN ACID?

The fumes that pour out of a car's exhaust-pipe don't smell very nice, do they? Well, one of the two kinds of gases that make rain acid comes from car exhausts when the engine is running. They are called **nitrogen oxides**, and are made when petrol is burnt in the engine to make the car go.

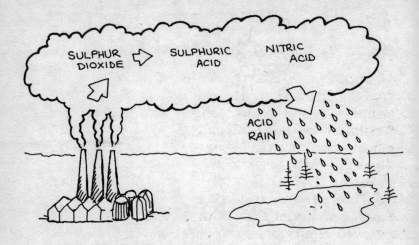

Nitrogen oxides also come from **power-stations** as they burn lots of coal or oil to make electricity for millions of people to use at home or at work. The other kind of gas that makes rain acid pours out of power-stations as well – it is called **sulphur dioxide**.

These gases float up into the sky, mix with the tiny drops of water that make up clouds, and turn into **sulphuric acid** and **nitric acid**. These strong, vinegary liquids fall to Earth as acid rain or float down as snow, mist, dust or fog.

Blowing in the wind

In 1985, 4 million tonnes of sulphur dioxide and nitrogen oxides (that is about the weight of 1 million elephants!) were pumped into the air in Britain. Every year, three-quarters of them are blown to other places in Europe. Because of this, Britain is called the 'Dirty Man of Europe' by the other countries.

Smoke and fumes from the USA are also blown over *its* neighbour. Out of the 12 million tonnes of acid that rain down on East Canada every year, over half comes from the USA. Many lakes, rivers and trees in Canada have already been poisoned. If nothing is done, its most famous tree, the maple, and the delicious syrup it gives us, could be gone for ever in ten years' time.

This kind of pollution has even reached as far as the North Pole – the snow and ice is not pure white any more, and there is a dirty, brown mist in the sky.

FOUR WAYS TO FIGHT BACK

1 You can help by using less electricity. Almost half of all the electricity we use now could be saved if all of us switched off things like lights, televisions or computers when they weren't being used, and made sure that buildings weren't wasting heat by being draughty. If we wasted less electricity, power-stations would not have to burn so much coal or oil to make it, and so there would be less smoke and fumes floating up into the sky.

2 Walk and cycle whenever you can. This gives you exercise and makes no pollution at all. Travel by bus or train instead of by car whenever you can. A lot of people sharing one bus or train makes much less pollution and traffic than if all those people travelled in their own cars. More people would use buses and trains if they were cheaper, safer and cleaner. This is something that the government can do.

3 Cars need to have their exhaust fumes cleaned. A special part called a **catalytic converter** that cleans exhaust fumes can be fitted to car exhaust systems. All cars in the USA are already fitted with catalytic converters because the government made a law saying that they should be.

4 The smoke and fumes that pour out of power-stations can be cleaned before they get into the air. This can be done by things called **scrubbers**. Scrubbers work by taking out the gases that make acid rain. The governments of Japan and Germany are two of the few governments in the world that make their power-stations do this.

CHAPTER 5
Waste

WHAT A WASTE!

Waste is another word for rubbish. It is a good word because most 'rubbish' is useful and we are wasting it by throwing it away. In Europe, over 5 million dustbinfuls of 'rubbish' are thrown away every day. Most other rich parts of the world are just as wasteful.

In poorer countries, people have much less, so much less is wasted.

WHAT'S IN A BIN?

Lift up the lid of most dustbins in Europe or North America and you will usually find: newspapers, bags, cartons, cereal boxes and egg boxes; plastic pots, bags,

52

bottles and tubs; glass bottles and jars; tins, cans and foil wrappers; fruit and vegetable peelings, pips and stones, meat and fish bones, and left-overs from meals; unwanted clothes; broken toys; dust and dirt.

If you lifted up the lid of most dustbins in South America, Africa or Asia you would see just how little is wasted. Most food is bought fresh in markets without lots of wrapping, so there are very few bags, jars or tins to throw away. There are hardly any left-overs from meals because often there is not enough food. Many people go hungry. Any food scraps are fed to animals or made into fertilizer to spread on fields. There are few unwanted clothes – old ones are woven into rugs or wrapped around people's feet because shoes are too expensive.

WHERE DOES IT ALL GO?

In many rich countries, 'rubbish' is collected and dumped, buried in soil, or burnt in special places called **incinerators**. A lot of litter and 'rubbish' is also just blown around towns and the countryside, often ending up in a river or sea. 'Rubbish' is even being washed up as far away as the South Pole!

WHERE DOES MOST OF IT COME FROM?

When we chuck out 'rubbish' we are not just getting rid of useless things. We are really throwing away precious stones, metals and fuels; trees, forests and lakes!

Paper and cardboard

These are made from wood, which comes from trees. It takes over 2 tonnes of wood to make 1 tonne of paper. Making paper also uses up lots of water and fuel, and chemicals that make pollution.

About 356,000 trees are cut down to make the paper and cardboard used in Britain in just one day. People in the USA use about 1 million tonnes of paper in just one week.

Plastic and foam

There are over fifty kinds of plastics, all made from oil, gas or coal found deep under the ground. The kind of foam used to make throw-away cups or hamburger boxes, and to pack delicate things, is also made of plastic. It feels light and spongy because strong chemicals called **chlorofluorocarbons** (CFCs for short) are added to it.

Scientists think that if we go on using up oil and gas so fast, there could be none left by the time you are as old as your grandparents. One day, coal will run out too. Every day, people in Britain chuck away about 7,000 tonnes of plastic. Every day, 60 million plastic bottles are used in the USA.

When natural things like wood, paper

or food are thrown away, they are broken down into little pieces by tiny germs in the air, water and soil, or eaten by insects and animals. In time (a few days for food scraps, longer for paper and wood), most of these things rot away and are turned into new soil. Things that rot away like this are called **biodegradable**.

Plastic and foam do not rot when they are thrown away – they are not biodegradable. They stay in one piece and cannot be broken down into new soil. Animals often choke on plastic and foam. They also get trapped in plastic rings that are used to hold tins together. If you snip these rings before you throw them away, you could be saving an animal's life. Another danger with foam is that it looks like food to some sea animals. When they swallow it, they float too much and cannot go under the water to feed or dive to safety.

When some plastics are burnt on bonfires or in incinerators they make air pollution. When foam is crushed or burnt, CFCs escape into the air – this is very dangerous (see chapters 7 and 8).

Glass

Glass is made from sand, limestone and soda ash, which melt when they are heated. This mixture is then made into different shapes, like bottles, jars and flat sheets for windows. When it cools, it is clear and hard.

Making glass uses up lots of water and fuels, and adds to pollution. In Britain, over 16 million glass bottles and jars are thrown away every day. In the USA it is 75 million!

When we throw glass away, it breaks, becoming a danger to people and animals, but it does not break down into new soil. It is not biodegradable.

Metals

Metals are mined out of the ground. If there is a forest in the way, the trees are destroyed. Mining is dangerous and expensive. It also pollutes rivers and lakes.

Metals go from the mines to factories, where they are made into things like cars, weapons, steel saucepans, iron pipes or aluminium cans. All this uses up lots of fuel and chemicals that make pollution. Every day, people in Britain throw away over 15 million empty food tins. Every day, people in the USA use 178 million aluminium drink cans.

Most metals are not biodegradable. Some rust away very slowly, becoming a danger to people and animals.

HOW TO GET RID OF WASTE

❶ Don't be wasteful

Long ago, before things were made by machines, it was hard to be wasteful because:

● everything had to be made by hand.

- people only made things that were really needed, and they were made to last because making things by hand is hard work.
- there were less things to buy because making things by hand is also much slower.
- people were poorer and the shops were not full of cheap things that they could run out and buy.

Since the Industrial Revolution, most things have been made by machines. This has made it easy for us to be wasteful because:

- the shops are full of things to buy.

BUY NOW!

BARGAINS!

0% INTE

● more people can afford to buy them.

WE'D BETTER BUY A NEW ONE!

● things are no longer made because people really need them. They are made to make money.
● things are not made to last. If they did last, who would buy the millions of new things that machines make so easily and quickly every day?
● many things are no longer mended when they go wrong because the people that make them get more money by selling brand-new fridges, cookers and so on than by selling parts to mend old ones.
● most people have a lot more, so a lot more gets thrown away.

60

So watch out! Here are some questions that will help you not to be wasteful:

Do I really need this? Ask yourself this before you buy something. It is a way of cutting down waste before you have even made any!

Does it have too many layers of wrapping? Ask yourself this when you pick up something to buy. If it does, don't buy it. It is a waste of cardboard, plastic, and so on.

Can I use this again? Ask yourself this when you are about to throw something away. The pots, jars and boxes that our shopping comes in can be used to keep food or toys in, for example. You can also make things with them.

Does someone else need this? Ask yourself this next time you are wondering what to do with clothes or shoes you have grown out of, or toys you no longer want.

❷ Recycle

To **recycle** means using things that we usually throw away to make more things. Most 'rubbish' can be recycled. There are special recycling centres that can turn waste paper into new paper, broken glass into new bottles and jars, plastics into plastic pieces for mending roads, metals into new cans, nails, and so on; and even old rags and wool into new cloth.

Recycling glass cuts down on pollution because it takes only half the fuel that it takes to make new glass. Recycling aluminium cans cuts down on even more pollution – it saves nearly *all* the fuel needed to make new cans. Recycling half of all the paper used in the world would save a forest the size of Ireland from being chopped down.

In Germany, recycling is made easy

because lorries pick up the paper, glass and metals from people's homes and take them to recycling centres. But in many other countries, people who want to recycle things have to make a special trip to a paper, bottle, rag or can bank – it's worth it, though. So recycle, and buy recycled things – oh yes, and don't be a litterbug!

CHAPTER 6

Toxic Pollution

Toxic means poisonous. There are two kinds of **toxic pollution**. One comes from different poisons made to kill living things like germs, weeds, mosquitoes, slugs, rats, or even (in wartime) people. These poisons are put into the air, water or food on purpose, but they often end up poisoning more people, animals or plants than they were meant to kill.

The second kind of toxic pollution comes from very strong chemicals used in factories to make a lot of what people buy, and from some metals and fuels. They are not made to kill or hurt living things, but they do when they are not used or got rid of carefully. Sometimes they escape into our air, water or food by accident. Other times, they are dumped there because it

seems the quickest, cheapest way to get rid of them.

Both kinds of toxic pollution are hurting or killing plants, animals and people all over the world.

Polluted penguins
South Pole penguins are being poisoned by chemicals used to kill insects in countries thousands of kilometres away. These chemicals (**pesticides** and **insecticides**) are sprayed on fields, washed by rain into rivers and seas, and carried by waves around the world.

White paper kills
The real colour of paper is brown, not white. Very strong chemical bleaches are used to make books, nappies, tissues, toilet paper and lots of other things look white.

Millions of litres of toxic waste from paper factories are being pumped into rivers, lakes and seas, often getting into drinking water. This waste (called **dioxin**) can give people and animals cancer as well as other illnesses. In the Soviet Union dioxin has polluted the biggest freshwater (drinking-water) lake in the world.

Sweden is one of the few countries that has stopped bleaching its own paper – but it still bleaches paper sold to other countries!

BUT, DAD– WHAT'S THE POINT IN **BLEACHING** THEM WHEN THEY END UP **THAT** COLOUR?

Jet-black poison

Oil is sometimes called 'black gold' because it is black and makes the people who sell it very rich. But it has also killed millions of birds and animals. In 1989, for example, a huge ship full of oil accidentally spilt millions of litres of 'black gold' into the sea, near Alaska (North America). Oil sticks together and floats, so all the oil that spilt from the tanker spread until the slick was thousands of kilometres wide. It killed 33,000 sea birds and 1,000 otters by sticking to their feathers or fur and poisoning them.

Not all oil gets into the sea by accident. When ships wash out their tanks, a lot of oil is dumped on purpose – 1 million tonnes of it every year!

Oil slicks only break up when they are sprayed with soapy chemicals. Then the oil mixes into the sea, but it is still poisonous, and can give people and animals illnesses like cancer.

Dangerous metals

Metals like mercury and **lead** are poisonous. In Japan, nearly 700 people died after eating seafood polluted with mercury that had been dumped in the sea for years by a chemical factory. Hundreds more people of all ages, but especially babies, were hurt by it.

Mercury is used to make batteries, thermometers, special lamps and engines. When these things are thrown away or burnt in incinerators, mercury escapes into the water and air. Most of the world's seas have been polluted by it. Mercury is also put into some pesticides.

Lead is not as poisonous as mercury but it too damages the brain and nerves. It collects slowly in the brain and makes children less intelligent. Some scientists think that it gives people cancer and other illnesses as well.

Most lead pollution comes from cars. It is added to petrol (except **unleaded petrol**) to make engines run smoothly. When petrol is burnt in an engine, lead

gets into the air through the exhaust pipe, and is breathed in by people. Every year, nearly half a million tonnes of lead are spat into the air by cars around the world.

When lead in the air mixes with rain and river water, it pollutes our drinking-water. The problem is made worse in places where old lead pipes are still used to carry water into people's homes.

Death on the Rhine

The Rhine is the biggest river in Europe. Hundreds of factories are built along it. They make almost a quarter of all the chemicals used in the world. Every day, poisons and metals like mercury and lead are flushed into the river from these factories.

Poisons also escape into the river because of factory fires and other accidents. In just one accident in 1986, half a million fish were killed. So far, nine different kinds of fish have been wiped out by toxic pollution.

Millions of people, including most of those in Holland, get their drinking-water from the Rhine.

Deadly gases, deadly weapons

If poisonous gases leak from a pesticide factory, for example, it can be very dangerous to people and animals nearby. This has not happened very often, but there have been a few accidents like this.

It is also very dangerous if poisonous gases are used as weapons in a war.

ALL OF US CAN HELP STOP TOXIC POLLUTION

Many shoppers do not realize that a lot of the things they buy are slowly poisoning the world. Washing-powders, cleaning-liquids, paints for decorating, and garden weed-killers are just some of the things that are full of toxic chemicals. As long as people go on buying them, business people will go on making them.

There *are* safer, more natural things that we can buy instead. They are made by business people who are trying to make money by keeping the world healthy. Special books called **green consumer guides** tell shoppers of all ages which things are safest to buy. Have you got one?

Governments can help by making better laws to stop things like factories and oil-tankers letting toxic pollution get into our air, water or food.

YES, BUT MY POWDER WASHES GREENER!

WHITER THAN WHITE POWDER

BIO-FRIENDLY WASHING-POWDER

CHAPTER 7

Global Warming

Globe is another word for planet. **Global warming** means that the weather of our planet is getting warmer. If you live in a cold country you might think that this is good. But for over 2 million years the temperature of the Earth has hardly changed.

If the weather around the world gets just a little warmer than it is now:

- the ice at the North and South Poles will melt.
- the seas will fill up with more water.
- many countries will disappear under the waves.
- cities like London, New York and Tokyo will be flooded.

- millions of people, animals and plants will drown.
- many more people will be made homeless.
- countries that now grow food will become too hot and dry to grow any.
- many people will starve.
- there could be more bad storms and hurricanes than ever before.

THE HEAT TRAP

Global warming is happening because too much heat is being trapped by pollution.

The sun warms up the Earth. A lot of the sun's heat 'bounces' off the ground and the air, and back into space. This is why the Earth does not get hotter and hotter, and why the temperature is just right for people, animals and plants to stay alive. Scientists have not found any other planet where the temperature is perfect for living things.

But now pollution in the sky is trapping some of the heat that warms up the Earth, and stopping it from bouncing back into space. This pollution is like the windows of a greenhouse. Like glass, it lets the sunshine in, but the heat inside cannot escape as quickly, and the greenhouse gets hotter and hotter. (Because of this, global warming

is also called the **greenhouse effect**.) The difference is that if it gets too hot in a greenhouse, you can open the door or windows. But with global warming there are no windows or doors to open – only heat-trapping pollution that will take years to go away.

Heat-trapping pollution is made up of lots of different kinds of gases. You have probably heard of the first two:

● **ozone**. When the sun's rays go through air pollution near the ground they make ozone. When nature makes ozone high up in the sky, it is very useful (see chapter 8). But when it is made near the ground, it stays there, trapping heat and harming plants.

- CFCs. As well as being used to make foam, CFCs are used in many aerosol sprays, fire extinguishers, fridges and air-conditioners. CFCs last longer than the other heat-trappers. Some may stay in the sky for over 20,000 years!

The other gases come from:

- fuels like oil, coal and wood when they are burnt to make electricity in power-stations, run cars or clear rain forests. This gas is called carbon dioxide, and more than 10 billion tonnes of it get into the air every year. Carbon dioxide makes up over half of all heat-trapping pollution.

- power-stations, factories, cars and chemical fertilizers. This gas is called nitrous oxide.

- sewage, rotting waste in rubbish dumps, cattle, and swampy rice-fields. This smelly gas is called methane.

HOW TO BEAT THE HEAT TRAP

Global warming is made from the pollution that comes from too many people having too many farms and cattle; making too much sewage; burning too many forests; using too much fuel in factories and power-stations to make things we do not really need; driving too many cars, and throwing too much away.

In other words, all the 'monsters' that you have read about so far add up to global warming. Because of this, the way to beat the heat trap is for governments and ordinary people to beat over-population, sewage, deforestation, acid rain, waste and toxic pollution.

We must start straight away because it will take a long time for all the pollution already in the sky to disappear. The Earth has already started to warm up. In the ninety years between 1900 and 1990, the five hottest years were all between 1980 and 1990, with 1990 being the hottest ever! Even if we stop making all heat-trapping gases right now, the weather around the world will still get a little warmer. There is no time to waste.

CHAPTER 8
Nuclear Radiation

Have you ever heard of the Stone Age? It was a time thousands of years ago when people began to use rocks and stones to make things, like arrowheads and tools. Later on, people learned how to make things from metals like bronze, so this age is called the Bronze Age. Did you know that *you* are growing up in the Nuclear Age? This is because, not long ago, people discovered that they could use something called **nuclear radiation** to make electricity and bombs.

Nuclear radiation is also used by doctors and dentists so that they can see if something is wrong inside your body. **X-Ray** pictures are taken by aiming a very, very tiny bit of nuclear radiation at a part of your body. The radiation will go through the skin but not through harder things like bones or teeth so they will show up in the picture and if anything's wrong, it can often be put right.

If people have a huge amount of nuclear radiation all at once, they get **radiation sickness** and will probably die after a few days. A little radiation every day for many years can give people a kind of cancer called leukaemia. Too much radiation is also dangerous for animals and plants.

You cannot feel, see or smell nuclear radiation. You need a special machine to tell you it is there. The most powerful rays can go through almost anything. Only a thick 'wall' of lead, steel or concrete can stop them. Because of this, nuclear radiation is one of the most dangerous kinds of pollution.

When something gives out nuclear radiation, it is **radioactive**. When something is radioactive, it can make other things radioactive.

WHERE DOES IT COME FROM?

The Sun
The sun and other stars in outer space give out a lot of nuclear radiation. The Earth is protected from nearly all of these deadly rays by a layer of ozone gas high

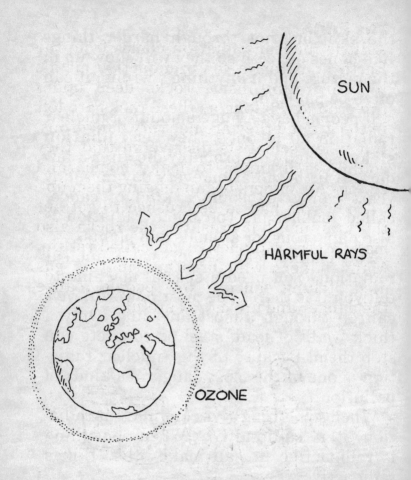

SUN

HARMFUL RAYS

OZONE

up in the sky. Scientists tell us that the **ozone layer** is getting thinner. This means that more dangerous rays are getting through. More people in Australia and North America are becoming ill with skin cancer than ever before. There is also a hole in the ozone layer over the South Pole that is as big as North America!

The Earth

A little nuclear radiation comes from the Earth and from a few radioactive metals like **uranium** inside rocks deep under the ground. As long as these rocks are left in the ground they are not very dangerous. But when scientists discovered that they could use uranium to make bombs and electricity, miners began digging them up.

The rocks had to be crushed to get out the uranium, but crushing the rocks also made a very radioactive gas called **radon**. Many miners who breathed in this gas died of lung cancer. Now people realize the danger and are more careful.

MAKING ELECTRICITY

Did you know that when you turn on a light, radioactive metals from under the ground might have helped to make some of the electricity you are using?

This is how it works. Scientists use complicated technology to make uranium much more radioactive in **nuclear power-stations.** When this happens, the uranium gives off enormous heat that is used to heat up water. The water becomes a powerful jet of steam that pushes turbines to make electricity.

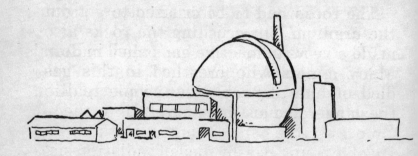

Nuclear power-stations are built with thick walls of steel and concrete to stop radiation leaking out. There are about 350 nuclear power-stations in the world, mostly in North America, Europe and Japan. They make a lot less than a quarter of the world's electricity.

Some of the uranium used to make electricity can be used again. But first it has to be taken to a special place called a **reprocessing plant**. The uranium is 'washed' with strong chemicals and sent back to nuclear power-stations.

THE RISKS OF NUCLEAR POWER

Accidents

Making electricity from **nuclear power** is very complicated. People can make mistakes. Things *do* go wrong. There have already been ten big accidents since nuclear power was first used over thirty years ago. After one accident in 1979, the USA stopped building nuclear power-stations.

The worst accident happened in April 1986. A nuclear power-station at Chernobyl, in the USSR blew up. The explosion sent lots of nuclear radiation into the air and over the land. Nuclear workers and people living nearby died of radiation sickness. An invisible 'cloud' was blown over northern Europe. Thousands more will die of cancer from the radiation.

Pollution and leaks

Nuclear power-stations and reprocessing plants let out waste gases and liquids which are a little radioactive. The Sellafield reprocessing plant in England, for example, pours 2 million tonnes of radioactive water into the Irish Sea every year. Other radiation pollution escapes in leaks. Many nuclear workers have been made ill by radiation leaks. More children living close to nuclear power-stations or re-processing plants become ill with leukaemia than children who do not live nearby.

Moving used uranium
If a train, lorry or ship has an accident while carrying very radioactive used uranium from nuclear power-stations to re-processing plants, nuclear radiation could pollute many kilometres of land, air and water, and kill many living things.

Radioactive waste
The waste from nuclear power-stations and reprocessing plants is also danger-ously radioactive. Like toxic pollution, if it is not got rid of very carefully, it can

kill. Unlike toxic pollution, **radioactive waste** goes on sending out deadly invisible rays for thousands, even millions of years. Radioactive waste is usually stored in steel and concrete, then buried deep under the ground or sea.

NUCLEAR POWER – GOOD OR BAD?

At first, scientists thought that nuclear power would give us cheap electricity without pollution. But:

- it costs billions of dollars to build nuclear power-plants.
- it is very expensive to get rid of radioactive waste.
- there is a big risk of pollution from accidents;
- uranium, like oil, gas and coal, will one day run out.

There are other ways of making electricity. Wind and waves can be used to turn turbines. Sunlight can be turned into electricity by 'sun batteries' called **solar cells**. The sun, wind and waves are free 'fuel' that will never run out and they make no pollution.

More and more people in the world

think it would be good to spend less money on nuclear power and more on **safe power**.

NUCLEAR BOMBS

You have seen how scientists use radioactive metal to make heat and power. They also use it to make **nuclear bombs** that are 20,000 times more powerful than ordinary bombs, and up to millions of times hotter.

When an ordinary bomb explodes, it blows up a car or even a large building if the bomb is very big. But if a nuclear bomb exploded, it could blow up a whole city; make enough heat to melt everything for miles around; give off lots and lots of radiation all at once; kill many people and

other living things; pollute the air, food and water with radiation for hundreds of years, and spread deadly radioactivity far from where the bomb exploded.

In 1945, at the end of the Second World War, the USA dropped two nuclear bombs on Japan that were much less powerful than the bombs made nowadays. But even those bombs killed 300,000 people straight away! Thousands more died soon after from radiation sickness, and others are still dying of cancer.

Today, even though only a few countries have nuclear bombs, there are enough to destroy every single city in the world fifty times. The bombs in just *one* of today's nuclear submarines have eight times more power than *all* the weapons used in the Second World War put together.

Like nuclear power, nuclear bombs cost billions of pounds. The money that it costs to build one nuclear submarine, for example, would buy all the things that school-children and teachers in twenty-three developing countries need in one year. Nuclear bombs are also very dangerous to make and to move from one place to another.

NUCLEAR TESTS

Since nuclear bombs were invented about fifty years ago, scientists have been testing them by blowing them up in deserts, seas and under the ground. When they realized the dangers of radiation, the governments of the USA, Britain and France started doing **nuclear tests** far away from their own countries. The USA, for example, exploded two nuclear bombs (in 1946 and 1948) near islands in the South Pacific. No warning was given, and many island people became ill and died.

In 1963, the USA, Britain, the USSR and 130 other countries agreed to test nuclear bombs only under the ground. China and France did not agree to this. France has carried on doing nuclear tests in the Pacific.

CHAPTER 9

Green Knights

There are many stories about how, long ago, knights in shining armour would ride out into the countryside and bravely fight fierce monsters or help people in trouble.

Today, we have got Dirty Great Monsters and a whole planet in trouble. We need all the knights we can get – everyone from girls and boys to grannies and grandads! Because green is the colour of healthy trees, fields and forests, people who care about keeping the Earth healthy are called **green**. You can become a 'green knight' by:

1 Sharing

2 Looking after what you've got

91

③ Using green consumer guides to shop safely
④ Buying only what you really need
⑤ Recycling used things
⑥ Being careful with litter
⑦ Walking and cycling
⑧ Saving electricity and fuel
⑨ Travelling by bus or train
⑩ Writing letters to businesses and governments

Here are the names and addresses of some green groups that are working to help people and governments everywhere to understand exactly what has to be done to get our planet out of trouble.

People who think that the work being done by these groups is important, and want it to continue, often become members by paying a few pounds each year. Others prefer to give some money (a donation). The money from all the members and donations is used to pay for the groups' projects, their bills and wages. Members also help in other ways, like taking part in these projects or offering to work without pay.

If you would like information from any

of these groups, it is a good idea to send an extra envelope with a stamp and your address on it when you write to them.

Animal Aid, 7 Castle Street, Tonbridge, Kent TN9 1BH

This group gives information about the way animals are treated in factory farming and tests for make-up, medicines and drugs. They have lots of ideas about what you can do to help.

Friends of the Earth (FoE), 26–28 Underwood Street, London N1 7JQ

If you want to know more about any green problem, from acid rain to toxic pollution, this is the group to get in touch with. For over twenty years, FoE has given facts and advice to people of all ages.

Greenpeace, 30–31 Islington Green, London N1 8XE

Greenpeace is famous for taking 'non-violent, direct action' to fight green problems. One example of this was when they sailed a Greenpeace boat close to where nuclear bombs were going to be tested at sea. They did this to try to stop the test taking place. Their daring protests are often reported on the news.

Intermediate Technology Development Group (ITDG), Myson House, Railway Terrace, Rugby, Warwickshire CV21 3HT

Many people in developing countries would be able to grow enough food and have safe water, fuels and homes if they had the right kind of technology to help them. The technology needed is not always expensive or complicated, but it takes time and money for experts to find the answer to each different problem. The ITDG is working to share our technology with people who need it.

National Federation of City Farms, The Old Vicarage, Fraser Street, Windmill Hill, Bedminster, Bristol BS3 4LY

If you live in a city and have always wanted to visit a farm and help to look after the animals, then this group can tell you where to find a city farm near you.

Oxfam, 274 Banbury Road, Oxford OX2 7DZ

You have probably seen Oxfam shops in the high street. This is just one of the ways in which this well-known international charity makes money for people in developing countries who need food, clean water and many other kinds of help.

The Royal Society for Nature Conservation (RSNC) and WATCH, The Green, Witham Park, Lincoln LN5 7JN

This group helps people to look after nature and wildlife in both town and country. WATCH has activities and projects for children.

World Wide Fund for Nature (WWF), Panda House, Weyside Park, Godalming, Surrey GU7 1XR

WWF has been working to save disappearing animals and the wild places where they live for over thirty years. It has lots of information and publishes books for children on green problems.

Index